A Cat's Life

First published by Parragon in 2010
Parragon
Queen Street House
4 Queen Street
Bath BA1 1HE, UK

ISBN: 978-1-4454-0456-1

Printed in China

A Cat's Life

inspiration for cat lovers everywhere

PaRragon

Bath · New York · Singapore · Hong Kong · Cologne · Delhi · Melbourne

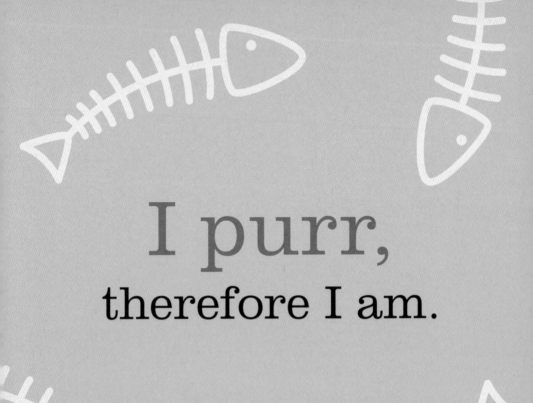

I purr,
therefore I am.

There are two means of refuge from the miseries of life: music and cats.

So much

time,

so little to do...

A meow
massages
the heart.

Kittens are angels with whiskers.

Dogs believe they are human.

Cats believe they are God.

What
greater
gift
than the love
of a cat?

A cats **worst** enemy is a closed door.

If only cats grew

into kittens.

The problem with cats is that they get the same exact look whether they see a moth or an axe murderer.

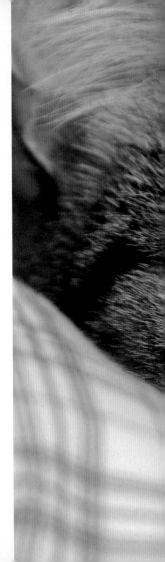

I believe cats to be

spirits come to earth.

A cat, I am sure, could

walk on a cloud

without coming through.

The dog for the man, the cat for the woman.

The smallest feline is a masterpiece.

In a cat's
world,
all things
belong to cats.

Cats only pretend to be domesticated if they think there's a bowl of milk in it for them.

Cats always seem
so very wise,
when staring with their
half-closed eyes.
Can they be thinking,
"I'll be nice, and
maybe she will
feed me twice?"

Isn't there always a cat napping on whatever you're reading?

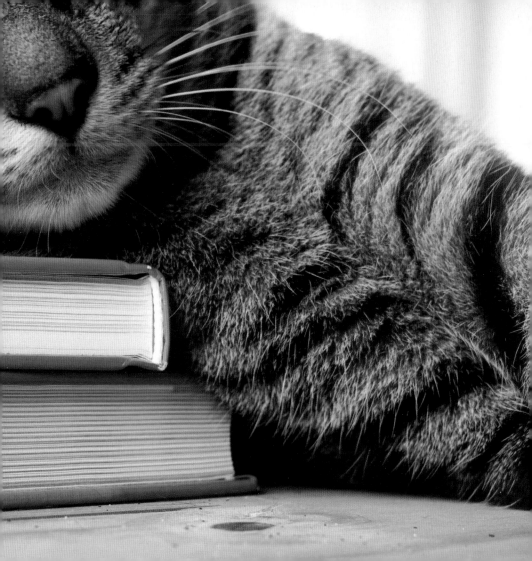

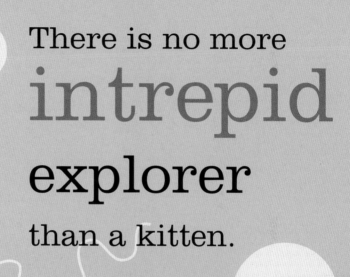

There is no more **intrepid** explorer than a kitten.

Thousands of years ago, cats were **worshipped as gods.**

Cats have **never forgotten** this.

The trouble with cats is that they've got no tact.

Her function is to sit and be admired.

A cat has absolute emotional honesty.

No matter
how much
cats fight,

there always seems to be

plenty of kittens.

Cats are
connoisseurs
of comfort.

To err
is human,
to purr
is feline.

Even the **stupidest** cat seems to know more than any dog.

One cat
just leads
to another.

Pussy cat, pussy cat
Where have u been?

I've been to London

To look at the Queen

Pussy cat, pussy cat
What did you there?

I frightened a little Mouse

Under her chair.

After scolding one's cat one looks into it's face and is seized by the ugly suspicion that it understood every word. And has filed it for reference.

People that don't

like cats
haven't met the
right one
yet.

Anything not nailed down is a cat toy.

It is

impossible

to keep a

straight face

in the presence of

one or more

kittens.

Two things are **aesthetically** **perfect** in the world -

the clock and the cat.

The
ideal
of calm
exists in a
sitting cat.

Cats are rather

delicate

creatures and they
are subject to a good
many **ailments**,

but I never heard of one who

suffered from insomnia.

For me, one of the **pleasures** of cats' company is their **devotion** to bodily **comfort.**

Cats can **work out** mathematically the exact place to sit that will cause most inconvenience.

I gave an order
to a cat, and
the cat gave it to
its tail.

Time
spent
with cats is
never
wasted.

Some people say man is the **most dangerous** animal on the planet. Obviously those people have never met an angry cat.

It's really the

cat's
house

we just pay the

mortgage.

I have **studied** many philosophers and many cats.

The **wisdom** of cats is infinitely superior.

A little **drowsing** cat is an image of a perfect beatitude.

He lives in the halflights in secret places, free and alone, this mysterious little great being whom his mistress calls, My cat...

The cat
is above
all things,
a
dramatist.

A cat's a cat and that's that.

Picture credits

Quote credits